American Events

THE ALL-AMERICAN GIRLS PROFESSIONAL BASEBALL LEAGUE

Trudy J. Hanmer

New Discovery Books
New York

Maxwell Macmillan Canada
Toronto

Maxwell Macmillan International
New York Oxford Singapore Sydney

Book design: Deborah Fillion
Cover photo courtesy of the National Baseball Library & Archive,
Cooperstown, N.Y.

Photo credits:
The Bettmann Archive: 4, 6, 16, 25, 26, 32, 35, 45, 48, 51, 52, 74, 75, 76, 78,
79, 80, 83, 84
National Baseball Library & Archive: 11, 15, 18, 19, 21, 29, 37, 38, 57, 58,
61, 62, 90

New Discovery Books
Macmillan Publishing Company
866 Third Avenue
New York, NY 10022

Maxwell Macmillan Canada, Inc.
1200 Eglinton Avenue East
Suite 200
Don Mills, Ontario M3C 3N1

Macmillan Publishing Company is part of the Maxwell Communication
Group of Companies.

First Edition

Printed in the United States of America

10 9 8 7 6 5 4 3 2 1

Library of Congress Cataloging-in-Publication Data

Hanmer, Trudy J.
        The All-American Girls Professional Baseball League / by Trudy J.
Hanmer. — 1st ed.
            p. cm. — (American events)
        Includes bibliographical references (p.) and index.
        ISBN 0-02-742595-9
        1. All-American Girls Professional Baseball League—History—
Juvenile literature. [1. All-American Girls Professional Baseball League.
2. Baseball—History.] I. Title. II. Series.
        GV875.A56H36 1994
        796.357'64'0973—dc20   94-1233
        Summary: The history of the All-American Girls Professional Baseball League,
which existed from 1943 to 1954.

0-382-24731-0 (pbk.)

For Judy, Kate, and Tasia:
past, present, and future ballplayers

Helen Fibarski of the Kenosha Comets is trapped between Dorothy Naum and Charlene Pryer of the Muskegon Lassies during an AAGPBL championship game.

CONTENTS

For young women like Jenny Fille, it took legal action to ensure that they were able to play on Little League teams.

Chapter 1

FOR BOYS ONLY

I n the early 1950s a young father from Long Beach, California, took his two children to see a major-league baseball game. Both of them fell in love with the sport. The boy, Randy, grew up to be a pitcher for the San Francisco Giants. His sister, Billie Jean, grew up to be a major-league athlete as well. But although she loved baseball, she had to choose a different sport. As Billie Jean King, world champion tennis player, she was the more successful athlete of the pair. But she could not play the sport she loved. As she wrote in her autobiography, "It was unfair of me to love it, I understood soon enough, because there was no place for an American girl to go in the national pastime."[1]

Billie Jean King was right about the absence of women in major-league baseball when she was entering sports. There was a time, however, when women could play national league baseball in major-league parks. If Billie Jean had been born 20 years earlier, she could have played baseball on a team in a professional league. From 1943 to 1954 the All-American Girls Professional Baseball League fielded a dozen "major-league" teams and even maintained a minor-league farm team system for training young women for the majors. For 12 seasons women took to the diamonds each spring when umpires called "Play ball."

Over the course of the 20th century, women have broken into traditionally male ranks in many fields, including sports. Women athletes have proved that they can attract both spectators and sponsors. The women's tennis circuit and the Ladies Professional Golf Association (LPGA) are arenas where women have demonstrated outstanding athletic ability and keen sportsmanship. Baseball, however, has remained mostly closed to women. Unlike tennis and golf, baseball is classified as a contact sport, along with football, hockey, and basketball, and women's right to play contact sports on the same basis as men is not yet protected under federal law. More important, however, is that baseball has traditionally been viewed as the province of men. The men who run professional baseball are not interested in sharing their pastime with women.

In the 1990s, in spite of the public disgruntlement over multimillion-dollar contracts, walkouts, and players' brawls and tantrums, baseball was still the number one sport in the United States, whether measured in number of fans or sponsors' dollars. For nearly two centuries baseball has ranked with hot dogs, apple pie, and the Fourth of July on the list of those things that define America. American parents can dream that their sons might grow up to be president, and American boys can dream of growing up to play for the Yankees or the Cubs or the Braves or the Cardinals.

But as with many American dreams, these have long had the possibility of becoming a reality for boys only. So far no girl has grown up to be president, nor has any girl played major-league baseball. Yet. Times are changing for American girls and women, and nowhere has the movement for gender equality been more visible than in the world of sports.

In the history of the women's movement, the fight to integrate girls into baseball holds significance far beyond the actual numbers of girls who have chosen to play the sport. When a six-year-old girl squaring off in T-ball can swing confidently, knowing as surely as her brother that only her skill and interest will limit her future in baseball, then and only then can the sport truly be called *All* American.

According to legend, a young West Point cadet, Abner Doubleday, invented the game of baseball in 1839. There have been many conflicting accounts of baseball's beginnings, but the fact is that by the 1830s the game of baseball was well entrenched in American society. The great supreme court justice Oliver Wendell Holmes recalled with great nostalgia the time he spent playing baseball at Harvard in 1829. Shortly after the Civil War, professional baseball started when paid teams began playing for paying customers. The Cincinnati Red Stockings of 1869 own the distinction of being the first professional team. By 1945 the Knickerbocker Club in New York City had printed a formal set of rules for the game (based on Doubleday's guidelines).

Baseball caught on quickly among American youth. Unlike cricket, its British counterpart, it did not require a lot of specialized equipment. As sports historian Mabel Lee has written, "By the mid–1870s all young America was playing the game in school yards, playgrounds, empty lots, wherever children could find a fairly good-sized spot and something to use for bats and balls."[2]

The early game did not look much like modern baseball. No players, not even the pros of Cincinnati, wore gloves until the 1870s, and until gloves entered the game, batters were out if the ball was caught on the first bounce. Only the diamond-shaped field and the nine-member team bore much resemblance to today's game. Bats, balls, distances along the base paths, and pitching techniques were all very different from those in use today. It was not until 1884 that overhand pitching became the norm,

For many years, women could watch, but not play, baseball, which was considered a sport only for men.

and until 1887 batters were allowed to call for a high pitch or a low pitch. The distance from the pitcher's mound to home plate was uniformly at 60′ 6″ in 1893. And not until 1889 was it universally accepted that four balls would equal a walk.

The beginnings of baseball coincided with the Victorian era in America. It was a time when women were definitely second-class citizens. Women neither voted nor sat on juries, and there were severe restrictions on their rights to own property, to sue for divorce, or to enter professions such as law, medicine, or engineering. Most men and a whole lot of women accepted the view that women were the weaker, more delicate sex. They needed protection and were shielded from anything that might be harmful, including physical activity.

Women were definitely not supposed to play "male" sports such as baseball. Sports provided an arena for men to demonstrate strength, courage, and skill, masculine traits also important in protecting women and children, another male role in those days. Contact sports were related to traditional male pursuits such as hunting and war, pastimes that usually excluded females. Because men are generally stronger and bigger and faster than women, it was easy to hypothesize that women—the frailer, gentler sex—would get hurt if they played with men or played men's games. As one historian of women's sports has summarized it, "Sex differences were reinforced and entrenched by excluding women from the 'manly' sports" and in turn reinforced "the notion that male physical superiority and male supremacy were inextricably linked."[3] In short, bigger was better.

Whenever girls or women demonstrated any interest in sports, they were told that their actions were unfeminine. Doctors—who were almost exclusively men—offered the opinion that women needed all their energy to bear children. (As late as 1936 a doctor writing in *Scientific American* explained that women's participation in sports would lead to "feminine muscular development" that would "interfere with motherhood.")[4]

As baseball became more and more popular in the United States, it was only natural that girls would want to play the game that had so captured the imaginations of their brothers. As early as 1867 an amateur team from Washington, D.C., the Nationals, traveled throughout the Midwest, playing teams in Cincinnati, St. Louis, Louisville, and Indianapolis. It was not unusual for a team to score more than 100 runs. Baseball looked like fun— and it was. Lots of girls wanted to play. They did not care that Albert G. Spalding, a sporting goods salesman whose name would be stitched into baseballs and gloves for over a century, had declared the sport "too strenuous for womankind."[5]

For many young men, college was the place to play team sports. Once again young women were excluded. Higher education was closed to most women during much of the 19th century. The exclusion of women from education and from the political life of the nation had begun to trouble many women. A few radicals, such as Susan B. Anthony and Elizabeth Cady Stanton, began to agitate publicly for an end to women's second-class status.

The reordering of American society brought about by the Civil War encouraged changing attitudes about women's roles. Now that black Americans, at least black men, were guaranteed equal rights as citizens under the Constitution, there were many Americans who believed that women also should have equal rights. To insure that women would be productive, intelligent citizens, these people argued that women needed access to a college education.

College and sports had long been synonymous. In 1859 the first college baseball game was played between Williams and Amherst colleges. For men the best college memories were often of their participation on a team. Increasingly, the sport they remembered most fondly was baseball. When women's colleges opened, sports were part of the curriculum right from the start. Within a year of its founding in 1865, Vassar College had two baseball clubs. At Smith College, founded in the next decade, baseball was an important activity right from the beginning, in spite of the awkward clothing the women had to wear. A Smith or Vassar batter "had to hit the ball, drop the bat, lift the train of her long skirt, drape it over her arm, and—if she wasn't already out—dash to first."[6]

Most men continued to take a dim view of women playing baseball. At the University of Pennsylvania five women tried to play baseball in 1904. The men in the administration banned them from doing so anywhere on the campus.

Despite the difficulties, college women continued to play for recreation, although not for a living. Beginning in the 1890s, however, a group of young women attempted to play baseball professionally. Called Bloomer Girls, after the first pants style worn by women, they usually came from working-class families. Since the beginning of professional teams, sports has been a way for young people—mostly men—to escape from poverty. Few children whose parents worked in the mills and factories of late 19th-century America could afford college. Sports was one of the few ways that they could escape the low-paying, back-breaking work that had trapped their parents.

Between the 1890s and 1920s, Bloomer Girl teams played baseball in the industrial cities of the Northeast and throughout the Midwest. Bloomer teams also included men. In the early years the catcher was invariably a man, and often three or four other men belonged to the team. Beginning in the 1920s, major-league teams owned minor-league teams where young men could get experience and move up to the majors. Before the invention of this system, the Bloomer teams provided a way for young male ballplayers to gain experience. Rogers Hornsby, a member of the Baseball Hall of Fame, got his first professional baseball experience on a Bloomer team.

Initially, men who played on the Bloomer teams wore wigs and skirts. Soon, however, the women playing Bloomer ball decided to wear men's

An early Bloomer Girls team

The costumes worn by the Daisies illustrate how the Bloomer Girls got their name.

uniforms because it was much easier to play ball in pants and shirts than in skirts or even the bloomers that gave the teams their name.

The Bloomer teams rarely played against one another. Rather, they played exhibition games, traveling around an area challenging men's teams to contests. Because they not only played a men's game but also played with and against men, Bloomer Girls had an unsavory reputation. Most middle- and upper-class American families thought it improper to attend Bloomer games. The women who played were equated with carnival sideshow "freaks."

In spite of their reputation, the ranks of the Bloomer Girls produced a number of women who made baseball history. On July 5, 1898, Lizzie Arlington pitched in a regular season men's minor-league game. Like so many of the Bloomer Girls, Lizzie grew up in a mining town, playing ball with her brothers. When she signed her contract to play for the Reading, Pennsylvania, team, she was offered $100 a week, double what her father earned in the Pennsylvania coal mines. The man who offered this contract to Lizzie Arlington, Edward Grant Barrow, later served as chief executive officer of the New York Yankees when Babe Ruth and Lou Gehrig played for that team.

Barrow was a promoter who hoped that big crowds would turn out to see a woman pitch. Such was not the case. The local paper reported: "Miss Arlington might do as a pitcher among amateurs, but the sluggers of the Atlantic League would soon put her out of business. She, of course, hasn't the strength to get much speed and has poor control. But, for a woman, she is a success."[7] Lizzie was sent back to the Bloomers, but she has the distinction of being the first woman to sign a contract to play professional minor-league baseball.

Another Bloomer Girl record setter was Lizzie Murphy, one of six children of a mill worker. She began working in the woolen mills as expected, but she dreamed of another life, one playing baseball. By the time she was 15 she was a paid player on a Warren, Rhode Island, team. By 1918 when she was 24, she had signed a contract to play with the semiprofessional Ed Carr's All-Stars of Boston. Lizzie Murphy continued to play with this team until 1935, when she retired as a ballplayer.

During her long career Murphy played all over New England in exhibition games. A major breakthrough for women in baseball came when Murphy played in Fenway Park in 1922. That year the Boston Red Sox played a charity game against an all-star team composed of players from the majors and the minors. Lizzie Murphy was chosen to play first base for the all-star team. Six years later Lizzie had her greatest triumph when she played with the National League All-Stars. In this exhibition game, played against the Boston Braves, Lizzie again played first base. In this 1928 contest she became the first woman to play for a major-league team in an exhibition game. In spite of her accomplishments, at the end of Lizzie's baseball days, when she was 41, there was no retirement package. She had to return to the life of manual labor she had hoped to escape, once again working in the mills of New England.

Lizzie Murphy

Yet a third mill girl who achieved success in Bloomer baseball—and whose life ended more happily than Lizzie Murphy's—was Mary Gilroy Hockenbury. Born in Philadelphia, Mary Gilroy had seven brothers and three sisters. Like Lizzie Murphy, she was working in the mills with her parents by the age of 12. The yarn factory where she worked sponsored a Bloomer team—the Fleisher Bloomer Girls. Mary Gilroy quickly gained a reputation for her hitting. Two national teams, the New York Bloomer Girls and the Chicago All-Star Athletic Girls, tried to recruit her. After barnstorming (traveling from place to place) for one season with the Chicago team, Mary returned home and married a minor-league pitcher. She raised seven children, and three of her sons played minor-league ball. They all attributed their success to their mother. As one of them reminisced, "Mom would have a catch with us. It was great. The other kids in the neighborhood envied us."[8]

Two other heroines of the Bloomer Girl era were Jackie Mitchell and Edith Houghton. Mitchell signed a minor-league contract to play with the Chattanooga Lookouts, and in a 1931 exhibition game with the Yankees struck out both Babe Ruth and Lou Gehrig. Houghton, the youngest in a family of ten children, was playing shortstop for the Philadelphia Bobbies by the age of 13 and found that it gave her the opportunity to travel across the United States and even to Japan, where the Bobbies played exhibition games in the 1920s. After the demise of the Bobbies and a stint with the WAVES in World War II, Edith became a scout for the Philadelphia Phillies, the first woman to hold such a job.

Edith Houghton

The Bloomer Girl organizations all provided women with the opportunity to play ball, but the most successful teams also provided women with the opportunity to go into business as team owners and managers. Although most of the Bloomer teams were owned by men, two of the most successful Bloomer owner/managers were women. From World War I until the Great Depression the greatest of the Bloomer Girl teams—the New York Bloomer Girls, the Chicago All-Stars, and the Western Bloomer Girls—were owned and managed by either Margaret Nabel or Maud Nelson. Although both started as ballplayers, they reached their greatest fame and success as owners.

From 1920 to 1933 Margaret Nabel ran the New York Bloomer Girls exclusively. On the other hand, Maud Nelson owned and managed many teams, including Chicago and Western. A real entrepreneur, she recruited nationwide for the top players. Almost all her Bloomer teams carried three men on the roster (usually the catcher, the shortstop, and an outfielder), and she had an eye for gimmicks that would attract spectators. As one of her players, Margaret Gisolo, recalled, Nelson would hire a band to meet the team when it arrived in town and precede the players to the ballpark. The band music stirred people to follow the team. After Nelson had built up a team to where it was successful and had a loyal following of fans, she would sell it. By doing so, she created many teams and more opportunities for young women to play baseball.

Perhaps the most famous athlete to come through the ranks of Bloomer ball, however, was the legendary Babe Didrikson Zaharias. Born Mildred Ella Didrikson, during her childhood she was nicknamed Babe after Babe Ruth because she was such a good hitter. An accomplished athlete in many sports, Didrikson competed in the 1932 Olympics and was a medalist in three events—javelin, high jump, and hurdles. She wanted to be a professional athlete, however, but in the 1930s there were no professional oppor-

Babe Didrikson Zaharias practices with Burleigh Grimes of the St. Louis Cardinals.

tunities in track and field. Didrikson turned her skills to baseball, which she had played since she was a child.

For several years Didrikson toured with an otherwise all-male barnstorming baseball team, the House of David. In 1934 she earned $1,000 a month, a huge sum, especially for a woman, considering this was the height of the Great Depression. During exhibition games Didrikson pitched against both minor- and major-league players. She said of her pitching, "I couldn't seem to throw the ball past these major-leaguers."[9] Knowing that she had no future in major-league baseball, Didrikson became a professional golfer in 1936. Her popularity and her success gave the floundering Ladies Professional Golf Association the boost it needed to take its place in the world of competitive sports. LPGA members went on to become leading moneymakers in the field of professional women's athletics.

The 1930s saw a great economic depression in the United States. Money for recreation was scarce and attendance at all sports competitions dropped off. The Bloomer teams came to an end. The New York Bloomer Girls, the Western Bloomer Girls, the Philadelphia Bobbies, the American Athletic Girls, and the All-Star Ranger Girls were history by the end of the 1934 season.

But money was not the only reason for their demise. Across America girls who wanted to play ball were being organized into softball leagues. Hardball was increasingly viewed as a boys sport. Softball was considered less strenuous and thus better for girls. City recreation departments, schools, colleges, and the Young Women's Christian Association busily organized softball leagues for girls with a yen for baseball. A few of the Bloomer Girls made the transition. Edith Houghton, for example, played several seasons with the Roverettes, a semipro softball team. Most of the Bloomer Girls, however, hung up their uniforms, convinced that the glory days of women's baseball were over.

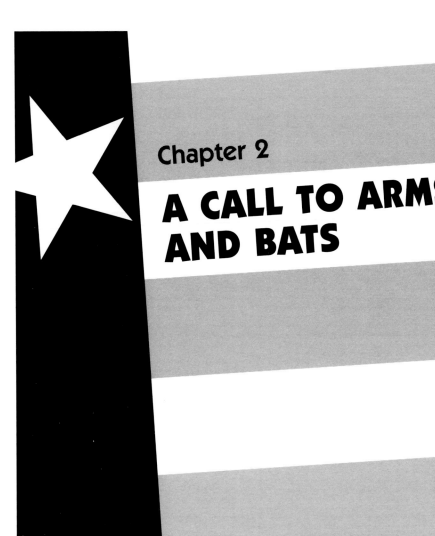

Chapter 2

A CALL TO ARMS . . . AND BATS

I n 1934, the year that the last of the Bloomer teams disbanded, the United States faced the worst economic crisis in its history. During the Great Depression there were those who even doubted that democracy and capitalism would survive. Attendance at baseball games hit all-time lows. What little money people earned was needed for food, rent, and clothing for their children. Baseball was a luxury they could not afford.

In 1934 the unemployment rate was 21.7 percent, three times more than in 1993. More than one out of every five Americans who wanted to work could not find a job. Many people believed that the few jobs that were available belonged to men. In most states laws were passed prohibiting married women from working. The assumption was that men were traditionally the breadwinners in a family, and that married women who worked were taking jobs away from men who needed them more. One state, Louisiana, even passed a law prohibiting any woman, married *or* single, from working. (This law was quickly declared unconstitutional.) In short, at a time of national crisis, women were expected to help by removing themselves from the competition for jobs. As in the 19th century, they were viewed as second-class citizens.

During the Depression, many women were unable to find work, as available jobs were most often given to men.

The Depression came to an end when the United States faced a new crisis. In 1939 Germany went to war against England and France, our traditional allies. Throughout 1940 American factories geared up to provide arms and ammunition for the English and the French. In 1941 Germany's ally Japan bombed the American naval base at Pearl Harbor, Hawaii, and the United States entered the war on the side of the Allies. By 1943 all of America was engaged in the mighty struggle to win World War II. Thousands of American men went to war. Factories all over the United States worked 24 hours a day to produce the planes, ships, uniforms, ammuni-

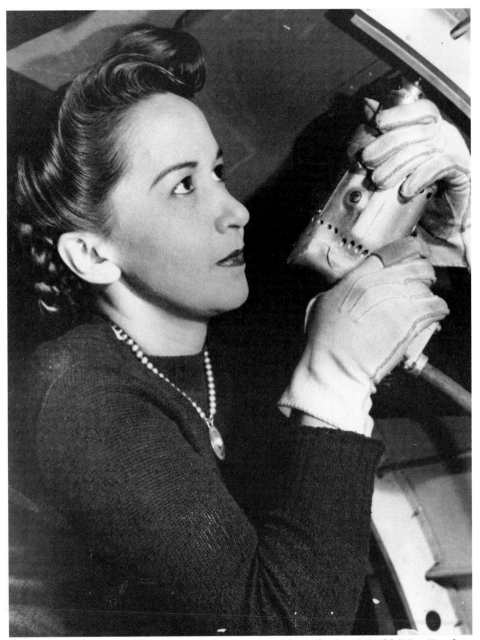

"Rosie the Riveter" became a symbol of patriotic duty during World War II, when women were expected to take over jobs usually held by men.

tion, and weapons needed for the sailors and soldiers fighting in the Pacific and Europe. Now there were more than enough jobs for everyone—including women.

All Americans, not just those fighting, were asked to make sacrifices. At home, certain foods and materials were rationed so that the fighting troops would have enough. Families were allowed to have 28 ounces of meat per week, 4 ounces of butter, and 4 pounds of cheese. Limits were also placed on flour, fish, sugar, and coffee. Each person was allowed three new pairs of shoes a year. No one could buy new sneakers because the rubber was needed to make tires for airplanes and jeeps. No new cars or tires were available, and gasoline was rationed. Recycling began. Nylon, silk, tin, metal, paper, and rubber were all needed in the war plants, and children and housewives became collectors of all kinds of scrap that could be re-used in the factories.

Once again women were asked to sacrifice. During the Depression they had been asked not to work. Now they were asked to leave their homes and families to perform jobs in factories that had always been off-limits to them. Women became electricians, welders, carpenters, steamfitters, plumbers, and mechanics. Because so many men were in the armed forces, there were not enough men at home to fill these jobs, which had traditionally been "men's work."

In the past, women had been told that they were not strong or mechanically skilled enough to do the work they were now being urged to do. Public opinion about women's abilities would have to be changed if women were to leave their housekeeping roles and work outside their homes. A public relations campaign was sponsored by the government to convince women that it was their patriotic duty to take a factory job. Rosie the Riveter became the symbol of working women in wartime. Attractive and feminine, Rosie, with her red lipstick and nail polish, was a welder who could do anything a man could do—at least in this national emergency. Her idealized face was invariably portrayed with her welding hat flipped up at a jaunty angle, the better to see her rosy cheeks, red lips, and flashing eyes.

In this climate many major-league athletes found themselves in a difficult position. In some ways it was a golden time for baseball. Many of the greatest players of all time were breaking major-league records—Stan Musial, Joe DiMaggio, and Ted Williams, for example. To some people, however, it seemed as though these healthy male athletes should be in uniform, fighting for their country, not at home playing games.

The baseball leagues were sensitive to this criticism. Because of gasoline rationing and restrictions on transportation (trains were needed to carry troops to the coastal ports where ships took them to Europe and the Pacific), the major-league teams held spring training in the North in 1943 rather than in Florida, which would require travel that would use precious resources like gasoline and train seats needed by the armed forces.

Still, the baseball commissioner, Kenesaw Mountain Landis, considered the possibility that major-league baseball should stop for the duration of the war. He sought the advice of President Franklin D. Roosevelt. Because of Roosevelt's reply, several ball players suggested electing him to an honorary place in the Baseball Hall of Fame at Cooperstown, New York. The president wrote to Landis, "I honestly feel that it will be the best for the country to keep baseball going. . . . Everybody will work longer hours and harder than ever before. That means that they ought to have a chance for recreation and for taking their minds off their work. . . . These players are a definite recreational asset to . . . their fellow citizens—and that in my judgment is thoroughly worthwhile."[1] Congress agreed with the president. They voted that baseball players could be drafted but that major-league ball should continue.

One person who worried a great deal about the future of major-league baseball during wartime was Philip K. Wrigley, the owner of the Chicago Cubs. Wrigley was a multimillionaire who had inherited his family's chewing gum business. He was extremely patriotic. As soon as the Japanese bombed Pearl Harbor, he sent all the aluminum in his factories (which he had stockpiled for use in gum wrappers) to the government to make planes. During the war, when sugar rationing made it difficult to make top-quality gum, Wrigley ordered his factories to make two kinds of chewing gum. The best kind was sent overseas, and the other kind, with less sugar and less flavor, was sold to Americans at home.

Attendance at Cubs games was low, and Wrigley worried that people

Philip K. Wrigley established the first organized women's baseball league. Ironically, as owner of the Chicago Cubs, he voted to keep black players out of major league baseball.

whose sons and brothers were fighting overseas did not like watching able-bodied men, who could be fighting, play ball. Furthermore, with gasoline rationing it was difficult for families to justify traveling to ball games when cars were supposed to be used for necessary travel only. Finally, the work week had been extended to a minimum of 48 hours. Even people who lived close to ballparks had very little leisure time to attend ball games.

Wrigley had long been aware of women's interest in baseball. In fact, throughout the 1930s he had declared that every Friday would be Ladies Day at Chicago's Wrigley Field where the Cubs played. Women were given special ticket prices and prizes or incentives to attend Cubs games. In 1943 Wrigley decided to emulate Rosie the Riveter, but not in his chewing gum factories. He decided to recruit women to play baseball. If women could become welders and plumbers during the war, then they could play ball, too. By playing ball women could provide inexpensive entertainment for exhausted factory workers on their few days off.

Wrigley decided that the best place to build these teams would be in the small industrial cities outside of Chicago and throughout the Midwest. The population in these cities had grown dramatically when their factories geared up for war production. However, the people were too far away from Chicago to be able to afford the time—or the gasoline—to get to the big city to see major-league ball. This area, in the heartland of America, had a long-standing commitment to baseball. As early as 1866 a four-state baseball tournament had been played in Rockford, Illinois, one of the cities Wrigley asked to sponsor one of his teams.

In the beginning Wrigley wanted the women to play softball. The game had increased in popularity among women and girls throughout the 1930s. By 1935 *Time* magazine estimated that more than two million Americans belonged to softball teams. Many of these players were men, but a lot of them were women. Many companies sponsored their own teams and even offered to pay higher salaries to good players who worked for them. This was true in Canada as well as in the United States. As his plan unfolded, Wrigley sent scouts to industrial cities in both countries to recruit the best women softball players.

The game that Wrigley envisioned was really a cross between softball and baseball. He thought that softball was not exciting enough to attract a crowd but that men's baseball might be too difficult for women. While the distance between bases in softball is 60 feet (18 meters) and in baseball 90 feet (27 meters), Wrigley's rules split the difference, setting the base paths at 70 feet (21 meters). Softball teams fielded ten players; Wrigley's teams would field nine, as in regular baseball. The ball used by Wrigley's teams was approximately 12 inches (30 centimeters) in circumference, slightly smaller than a regulation softball but somewhat larger than the regulation baseball. The games lasted nine innings, as did baseball games. The only exception was the first game of a doubleheader, which was seven innings, the traditional length of a softball game. The pitcher threw under-hand, as in softball, from a distance of 43 feet (13 meters). As *Newsweek* magazine reported, the new game fell "midway between softball and base-ball."[2]

The news went out across the Midwest and Canada that Wrigley was forming an All-American Girls Softball League. He chose the name care-fully. "All-American" emphasized the spirit of patriotism that was sweep-ing America and Canada, and the game to be played was closer to softball than baseball. Wrigley also knew that to make the game acceptable, he did not want any comparison with the Bloomer Girls and their carnival repu-tation. Although the Bloomer teams had provided opportunities for women to play baseball, they had always been a bit of a sideshow. "Nor-mal" women would not want to play that kind of ball. As Wrigley said, "We will select the kind of players that people will want to see in

Once news of Wrigley's baseball league spread, women lined up across the country to try out for the new teams.

action. . . . It won't be like the bad old days of peep shows and Bloomer Girls."[3] And although most of the players were over 18, they were always called girls, not only by Wrigley and the managers, but also by their fans.

Some of the prospective players read about the new league in the newspaper. This was the case for Canadian Mary "Bonnie" Baker, who would become a league star. As she recalled, "I was in the coffee shop I went to every morning before work, and I opened up the sports page and there was a picture of Mrs. Wrigley . . . and a model with this uniform on. I read it and said to myself, 'Oh, God, it's happening. Now am I going to be lucky enough to get in?'"[4]

Other players were recruited by scouts who visited areas around Chicago. Racine and Kenosha, Wisconsin; South Bend, Indiana; and Rockford, Illinois, had all agreed to host the first teams. It was logical to try to recruit players from these cities and others their size that lay within a day's train ride from Chicago. The new recruits had their transportation paid to Chicago, where tryouts would be held at Wrigley Field. Sixty players would be kept—15 per team.

Most of the recruits had never been away from home. Because many were as young as 17 or 18, their parents were reluctant to let them go away with strange men to a big city. For Connie Wisniewski, the daughter of Polish immigrants living in Detroit, the biggest obstacle to playing ball was her mother. Mrs. Wisniewski "was from Poland, very old-fashioned. She said only bad girls left home."[5] Only when Connie threatened to join the army, an even more dangerous occupation in Mrs. Wisniewski's eyes, was she allowed to go.

Many of the players were farm girls who had never left their hometowns. Jane "Jeep" Stoll recalled her trip to Wrigley Field: "I had never ridden on a train. I sat up all night in a Pullman car because I didn't understand how the seat was going to be my bed."[6] Other players, excited at the idea of leaving home, became homesick when they reached their new surroundings. Sophie Kurys, who would eventually break all league records for stolen bases, nearly left the first day. Like Wisniewski, she was the daughter of Eastern European immigrants, and she went to Chicago from the small city of Flint, Michigan. As she later recalled, "It was raining when I got there. I told them I wanted to turn around and go back home. . . . The next day the sun was shining and I felt fine."[7]

Many of the girls loved baseball and at last had a chance to do what they loved as a way of making a living. As Pepper Paire, a recruit from California, said, "We thought we'd died and gone to heaven."[8] Until she joined the league, the biggest reward Pepper had ever received for playing ball was a bag of groceries.

The salary was a major incentive for joining Wrigley's league. He offered to pay the players anywhere from $50 to $125 a week, plus expenses, far more than what they could earn at factory jobs. Ten dollars a week was a good entry-level salary for a girl in a factory, and she had to pay all her living expenses out of that. A ballplayer making $55 a week could bank most of it since the league paid for her food, hotel room, and transportation. For many of the players the salary would enable them to help support their families and save money for a college education, which was beyond the reach of ordinary factory workers—girls or boys. This was true, for example, of Lois Youngen, who eventually used her baseball earnings to attend college. She not only attended college with her baseball wages, but also saved enough to go on to earn her doctorate. She later became head of Physical Activities and Recreation at the University of Oregon.

For catcher Irene "Tuffy" Hickson, playing ball was both fun and a chance to help her mother: Playing in the league "was a chance to get paid for something I would have done for free. . . . My mother needed my help

Three AAGPBL pitchers receive tips at spring training from former New York Giants player Dave Bancroft.

at home, but she knew how much I loved to play ball. . . . I sent as much money home as I could."[9]

Traditionally, jobs for women had paid very little. Teaching was one job that had been almost exclusively the province of women. Shirley Jameson, a teacher turned ballplayer, found that "my summer salary was more than I made teaching nine months a year!"[10]

The ballad of the All-American Girls Softball League reflected the theme of diversity among the players. The song, written by Pepper Paire, went this way:

> We are the members of the All-American League,
> We come from cities, near and far,
> We are Canadians, Irish ones and Swedes,
> We're one for all, we're all for one, we're All-American.

Even Spanish-speaking Cuban players were recruited for the teams.

In recruiting for the league, however, one group was left out—African-Americans. Although many young black women played on softball teams, none of them were recruited for the league.

In excluding black players, the league mirrored the practice of major-league baseball. Although baseball was an extremely popular sport among African-American boys and men, they were excluded from the major leagues. In 1920, the year Babe Ruth signed with the New York Yankees, a black baseball league was formed. Called the Negro National League, this league fielded a score of major teams and had a farm system of minor-league teams just like the American League and National League. Great players such as Satchel Paige, Jackie Robinson, and Hank Aaron played in the Negro National League. It was not until 1947 that Jackie Robinson became the first black American in the major leagues. Desegregation in baseball occurred when Brooklyn Dodger owner Branch Rickey signed Robinson.

Branch Rickey was one of Wrigley's closest advisers and most ardent supporters in the formation of the women's baseball league. But in 1943 neither Rickey nor Wrigley was advocating the recruitment of black women players. Rickey's bold step in signing Robinson would not be replicated in the women's league.

By excluding black women from the league, Wrigley and his scouts missed out on many great ballplayers. The standout, however, was Toni Stone. Born Marcenia Lyle Alberga, she grew up in St. Paul, Minnesota. A second baseman, Stone played in the Negro American League minors for a short time. She also played with the San Francisco Sea Lions, a barnstorming team, and the minor-league New Orleans Creoles. The latter team paid her $300 a month. On all these teams she played hardball, and she was the only woman. In 1953 she was signed to play second base for the Indianapolis Clowns, a position formerly held by Hank Aaron. That season she batted .243 and won the

Toni STONE
Female 2nd Baseman of
Negro American League
C L O W N S

Years after her days as the only woman to play major league ball, Toni Stone throws out the first ball during a matchup between the Dodgers and the Giants.

distinction of being the only woman to play in the segregated majors.

Toni Stone's prowess and the interest of other young black women in baseball had little impact on the All-American Girls Professional Baseball League (as the league would eventually be called), however. In 1951 the league's directors considered integrating the league but voted against it. The All-American opened doors for women, but only white women were invited to walk through.

Chapter 3

LIPSTICK AND LINE DRIVES

When Philip Wrigley assured future fans and potential supporters of his new league that it would not be like "the bad old days" of Bloomer Girls, he was anticipating one of the biggest obstacles that the women playing baseball would have to face. Social custom, tradition, myth, and even medical and scientific opinion characterized sports as "manly." Because this opinion was so widespread, any girl or woman who was a good athlete was subjected to all kinds of criticism. She was seen as abnormal and unfeminine and was accused of not liking boys. "Tomboy"— the nickname Toni Stone's friends and family called her throughout her childhood—was the nicest thing she might be called. And it was the assumption of most tomboys' friends and families that their love of sports was just a phase that they would outgrow as they got older. Few people thought that respectable adult women could play any sport for a living. Wrigley knew that he would have to counter public opinion if the women's baseball league were to be successful.

Rejecting athletics as a normal pursuit for women was a way of reinforcing men's position of power in a society primarily controlled by men.

For women to possess the strength, speed, and muscular flexibility characteristic of athletic ability challenged their historically subservient position in society. As one historian of women's sports has written, "Sporting ability was hardly compatible with women's traditional subordinate role in patriarchal society."[1] In the 1930s, even Babe Didrikson, the first female superstar, was analyzed as much for her looks and social life as for her athletic ability. In reporting on Didrikson at the 1932 Olympics, one observer noted, "She was the muscle moll to end all muscle molls, the complete girl athlete . . . a tomboy who never wore makeup, who shingled her hair until it was as short as a boy's and never bothered to comb it, who didn't care about clothes and who despised silk underthings. . . . She had a boy's body, slim, straight, curveless . . . she looked and acted more like a boy than a girl." The writer went on to assure his readers that Didrikson was nevertheless "in every respect a wholesome normal female."[2]

Wrigley's goal was to prove to fans that the girls in his league were "wholesome normal females." When Lil Jackson arrived from Nashville, Tennessee, for tryouts at Wrigley Field, she knew she would have to be more than a good ballplayer to make one of the teams. As she recalled, "Mr. Wrigley didn't want athletic chorus girls. He wanted hard-nosed ballplayers, but ladies."[3] Chorus girls, a common form of female entertainer at the time, were associated with loose morals and fast living. As a *Newsweek* reporter put it, league members "were chosen for looks as much as for long hits."[4] Officially, the players were chosen for a combination of "playing ability, appearance and character."[5] What this meant was that some excellent ballplayers were rejected by the recruiters. As *Time* reported, "several outstanding players" were turned down "because they were either too uncouth, too hard-boiled or too masculine."[6]

It was not enough for Wrigley to recruit girls whose looks conformed to society's ideas of feminine beauty. To insure that all the players would exhibit proper manners, ladylike deportment, and the most feminine appearance possible, he hired teachers from the Helena Rubinstein beauty organization to provide "charm school" classes for the players after practice every day. The players were instructed in makeup, hairstyling, and manners. They were taught which fork to use for which course in a meal, how to put on a coat, how to get in and out of a car, and how to charm dates.

Reporters who covered the league never failed to mention the charm school lessons. As reported in *Newsweek*, "They learned posture and etiquette, how to choose and wear clothes, how to apply cosmetics, and how to take a called strike like a lady."[7] Lil Jackson recalled that they "learned . . . how to carry on a lady-like conversation."[8] Pepper Paire recalled that "it wasn't easy to walk with a book on your head when you had a charley horse."[9] The women baseball players were given special tips about game preparation that no Yankee or Dodger ever had to learn—for example, to put soap under their nails before a game to keep them cleaner and never to take to the field without lipstick in place.

When the earliest recruits arrived at Wrigley Field, they found that they were to be chaperoned on and off the field. It was the job of the chaperone, a woman who accompanied each team, to make sure that the charm school procedures were followed. As Shirley Jameson left the dugout one day to bat in a crucial game, the chaperone called her back in: "Oh, my dear, you don't have your lipstick on."[10]

Wrigley made sure that newspaper and magazine reporters covered the manners lessons of his players by issuing press releases about the classes. As Ken Sells, the first president of the league, remarked proudly, "They proved that women didn't have to sacrifice their femininity to be standouts in what was then a men's world."[11] Ads for the first games stressed that the new girls baseball league was "Exciting, Clean Fun" to which one could "Bring the Family." The war theme was also evident in these posters: "Watch these girls take their rightful place in the American sports world, as women are doing in hundreds of other fields."[12]

Actual charm school classes were discontinued after a few seasons, but all players continued to receive beauty kits and how-to pamphlets written by Helena Rubinstein. She wrote them specifically for the ballplayers. The guides captured Wrigley's desire to blend feminine charm and athletic ability:

> The All-American girl is a symbol of health, glamor, physical perfection, vim, vigor and a glowing personality. Being included on the All-American roster is indeed a privilege to be granted only to those who are especially chosen for looks, deportment and feminine charm, in addition to natural athletic ability. The accent, of course, is on neatness and feminine appeal. This is true on the playing field, on the street or in leisure moments. Avoid using rough and raucous talk and actions and be in all respects an All-American Girl.[13]

The chaperones who accompanied each team were responsible for monitoring behavior off the field as well as in the dugout. From the very beginning, strict rules governed off-field behavior. *Life* magazine reported that the players "always wear feminine attire, cannot smoke or drink in public, cannot have dates except with 'old friends,' and then only with the approval of . . . the chaperone."[14]

The rules were included in contracts so that there could be no question about players' understanding of the league's expectations. There were fines for failure to follow league rules. A $50 fine was levied on any player who failed to appear in public appropriately attired, coiffed, and made up. Two hours after every game the players were scheduled to be in their rooms. Off the field the players were forbidden to socialize with players from other teams. The official rules, printed and handed out to all recruits, included the following:

1. Always appear in feminine attire when not actively engaged in practice or playing ball. At no time may a player appear in the stands in her uniform.
2. Smoking and drinking are not permitted in public places.
3. All social engagements must be approved by the chaperones.
4. All living quarters and eating places must be approved by the chaperones.
5. [Away from home] each club will establish a satisfactory place to eat and a time when all members must be in their individual rooms. In general, the lapse of time will be two hours after the finish of the last game.
6. In order to sustain the complete spirit of rivalry between clubs, the members of the different clubs must not fraternize at any time during the season.[15]

Although some players, like Pepper Paire, scoffed at the rules and charm school requirements, others understood that in the conservative atmosphere of the 1940s the emphasis on femininity was necessary if the league was to attract as many fans as possible. The president of the Racine team, Don Black, reminded his team, "Nobody is especially surprised or impressed if a rough, tough mannish looking babe shows some ability at sports. But to realize that a truly feminine creature can reach the top in one branch of athletic endeavor is refreshing and pleasing. Your fans want you

While they played rough-and-tumble hardball on the field, players of the AAGPBL were expected to conform to stereotypical ideals of femininity at all times.

to look and act like ladies and still play ball like gentlemen."[16]

Looking like ladies meant, in Wrigley's view, wearing skirts to play ball. And as much as the players understood the need to please the crowds, they did not like wearing skirts. Most of them had worn men's uniforms on their prior teams. As Sophie Kurys, whose specialty was stealing bases, a practice made far more hazardous by her uniform skirt, said, "They thought that having skirts would show that we were extremely feminine. . . . But I think all of us would rather have played in standard uniforms."[17]

It was not to be. "Short hems and long socks were de rigueur"[18] on the diamond when the league took the field, in spite of changing fashions elsewhere. The war, which had catapulted women into men's jobs, had also stimulated changes in their dress. Rosie the Riveter wore practical overalls as did many of her real-life companions in the wartime factories. For the first time teenage girls in large numbers wore pants during leisure time—rolled up jeans being their favorite. Movie stars such as Katharine Hepburn and Marlene Dietrich had pioneered sophisticated trousers for women. Shorts were accepted casual wear at the beach.

Fearing adverse comparison with the Bloomer Girls, Wrigley, however, decided that the players in his league would wear skirts. With the help of Mrs. Wrigley, a tunic-style uniform was designed. Available in green, blue, yellow, or peach, the short-sleeved dress buttoned up the front and had a flared skirt. Hems were officially limited to six inches (fifteen centimeters) above the knee. Long socks, rolled just below the knee, and a modified baseball cap completed the outfit. Not only was the uniform uncomfortable, it could be downright painful. Players who stole bases and had to slide often suffered serious burns called strawberries. Joanne Winter, a Racine pitcher, expressed the opinion of most of the ballplayers when she said, "If I'd had a brain and a seamstress, I would have changed [the uniform]."[19] But the uniforms stayed. A decade after Wrigley had abandoned the organization, the league still played ball in the uniforms he had ordered.

By the close of the recruiting session in the spring of 1943, the rules were set, the chaperones and managers were hired, and four teams donned their uniforms to play ball. In Racine they were called the Belles, in Kenosha the Comets, in Rockford the Peaches, and in South Bend the Blue Sox. True to plan, each team carried 15 players. All the managers were former major-league players, and all were men.

As the 1943 season got underway the Belles were coached by Johnny Gottselig, the Peaches by Eddie Stumph, the Comets by Josh Billings, and the Blue Sox by Bert Niehoff. Gottselig was the only one of the original managers to last more than two seasons. He was also the only one who had coached women players before. This was later true of Bill Allington, the highly successful coach of the Rockford Peaches. Although he had played minor-league ball, he had coached women's softball teams before coming to Rockford. Many observers chalked up his team's success to this prior experience. The best managers, however, agreed with Jimmie Foxx, who said to his players, the Fort Wayne Daisies, "You are true major leaguers in my eyes."[20] For many other managers, coaching the women was a poor substitute for coaching men, and they were waiting for the end of the war to get back into the majors.

In June 1943 the season opened, with the Racine Belles playing against the South Bend Blue Sox. A local paper reported the game this way: "A crowd of 683 cash customers turned out despite the cool weather, but the temperature was nothing compared to the chill they received from the two hours and thirty-five minutes of how *not* to play."[21] In spite of major-league managers and feminine uniforms, the modified softball game was not a hit.

Sophie Kurys, who would become the league record holder for stolen bases, slides into second base during one of the first league games, which were then more like softball than baseball.

For the rest of the 1943 season, Wrigley and his advisers worked on ways to make the game more appealing to crowds. First came a name change for the league. Sensing that women playing softball was not the novelty that women playing baseball would be, Wrigley changed the league name to the All-American Girls Ball League, then to the All-American Girls Baseball League, and finally to the All-American Girls Professional Baseball League.

Changing the name was not enough, however. The rules had to be changed as well. The distance between the bases was lengthened, as was the distance between the pitcher's mound and home plate. Meanwhile, the ball grew steadily smaller until it became a regulation hardball. And, of course, from the beginning the league allowed leading off base and stealing, two practices outlawed in traditional softball.

The rule changes were made to speed up the game and make it more exciting for spectators. In softball, with its bigger ball, no-stealing rule, and shorter distance from the pitcher's mound to the plate, games were often pitchers' duels with very low scores and very little base running. With the rule modifications, Wrigley's game was far more exciting. Runners, hitters, and fielders all generated plays that captured the crowd's attention.

Rule changes were not the only changes made to attract paying customers in the first seasons. Always the patriot and always the entrepreneur, Wrigley promoted the games with a number of gimmicks. Men and women in the armed services were admitted free if they wore their uniforms to the ballpark. To emphasize support for the war effort, the players marched onto the field before each game in a *V* formation—the classic victory sign. The teams played a grueling six-day schedule, with at least one doubleheader per week. In addition, games were scheduled late at night—11:00 P.M.—in order to meet the schedule of factory workers coming off the evening shift.

Perhaps the most famous night game was played in July when an All-Star contest pitted the best players from Racine and Kenosha against the best players from Rockford and South Bend. The night was notable not for the game, which the Peaches/Blue Sox won 16–0, but for the fact that this was the first game ever played under lights at Wrigley Field. One player, Dorothy Hunter, complained about the primitive lights: "The outfielders were dead ducks; the ball went up in the air and they didn't know where it was."[22]

Also instrumental in promotional efforts were the backers in the four small cities hosting the teams. Local businesses put up awards, local fife and drum corps entertained before the games, and war bonds were offered as prizes. Although Wrigley had put up $100,000 to found the league, businessmen in each of the four founding cities who had pledged more than $20,000 per franchise knew it was in their best interest to see the teams attract large crowds of paying customers.

At the end of the 1943 season Wrigley viewed his venture as a success. The four teams had played more than 100 games before 176,000 fans. Racine ended the season in first place. Not only had the recruits of 1943 turned into ballplayers, they had proven Wrigley's theory that people would pay to see women play baseball.

As he looked to the second season, Wrigley planned to expand the league by adding more teams. The year 1944 would see the addition of a team from Minneapolis, the Millerettes, and a team from Milwaukee, the Chicks. Only one survived. Minneapolis was too far away to be accommodated in the league schedule. The Millerettes were 400 miles (648 kilometers) from their nearest competitor—and the teams always traveled by bus.

Another problem for the Minneapolis team was the size of the city. Although Wrigley dreamed of one day having major-league women's baseball in major cities across the country, big cities were not successful franchises. Cities with populations of a quarter million or more did not provide the support that a league franchise needed. Milwaukee had a population of 590,000 at the start of World War II. Too many other clubs and activities

Two Racine Belles relax between innings.

Doris Sams, star pitcher of the Muskegon Lassies and 1947 Most Valuable Player of the AAGPBL, warms up before a game.

were competing for people's attention. The Milwaukee franchise was bought out by Grand Rapids, a small city compared to Milwaukee, after two seasons.

It had also been part of Wrigley's plans to start a team that could play in Wrigley Field when the Cubs were on the road. As a practical matter, he did not like to see his stadium stands empty. Although Chicago fielded hundreds of softball teams and was home to a highly competitive softball league, the All-American women's team begun in that city did not succeed. With four million people Chicago was simply too big to be a successful All-American town.

In the small cities where the teams were successful, the players were local heroines, and star players quickly gathered local followings. Popular players helped local businesses advertise their products, and in return local businesses gave players cash prizes and appliances for outstanding performances. The importance of the players to the hometown fans was spelled out in the players guidebook. Players were told:

> Because you are a ball player and a member of the team in your home town city, it is taken for granted that you will be popular and well known by sight. . . . Both younger and older people will be interested in you. . . . Be as friendly and as gracious as you possibly can on these occasions. . . . Don't be abrupt or rude to fans if you can possibly avoid it. Letting them feel that they know you, giving them a good impression through your speech and mannerisms, will help to make them regular and steady fans and will develop more "customers" for the League.[23]

Most of the players preferred the hometown friendliness of the small cities. Connie Wisniewski, who grew up in the larger city of Detroit, loved playing for Grand Rapids because "the people were so nice. . . . They recognized us every place; they knew you when you went to mass at church. If you stopped at a restaurant, they made sure you had good seats. No matter what you did, it was 'Hey, there go the Chicks.' We never got that in Detroit."[24]

By the end of 1944 the league was well established in its four base towns in spite of the failed experiments in larger cities. For Wrigley, however, the realization that the teams could not successfully expand to large urban areas ended his interest in the league. For the first two seasons the advertising for the league had been handled by a man named Art Meyerhoff. At the end of the 1944 season Wrigley sold the league to Meyerhoff for $10,000. Ken Sells was replaced as league president by Max Carey, a former star outfielder for the Pittsburgh Pirates who had managed the Milwaukee Daisies for its only season.

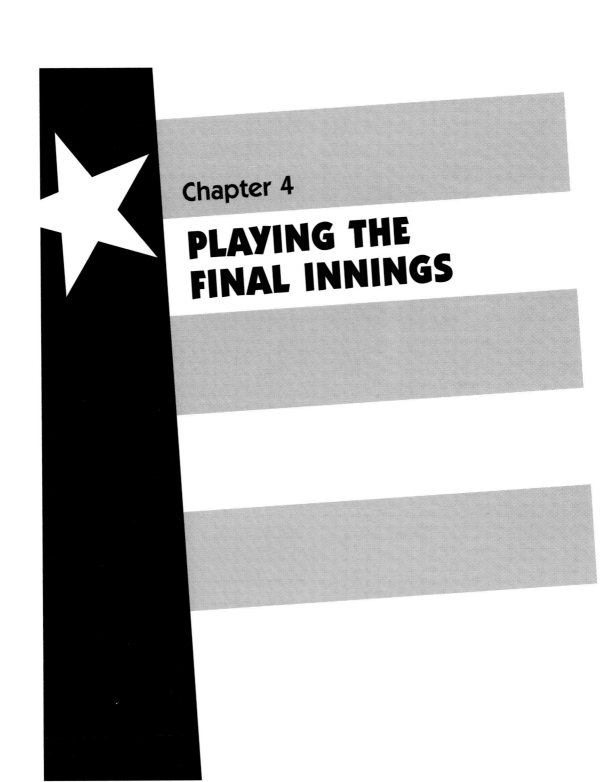

Chapter 4

PLAYING THE FINAL INNINGS

I n the 1930s Babe Ruth said of women: "They are too delicate. . . . It would kill them to play ball every day." During the Meyerhoff years, the players of the All-American Girls Professional Baseball League proved the Babe wrong. As the game changed to hardball, the teams attracted thousands of paying customers who were as enthusiastic about the records set by the women as they were about the records set in the major leagues by men.

Comparisons with men were inevitable, but the quality of play improved so dramatically that by the time Meyerhoff purchased the league, players had begun to receive high accolades from the male professionals who came to see them play. Chicago Cubs manager Charlie Grimm, watching Dorothy Schroeder play ball, said, "If she was a boy, I'd give $50,000 for her."[1] (At the time, Joe DiMaggio was earning $25,000 a year as a center fielder for the New York Yankees.) And Wally Pipp, the Yankees' first baseman, said that his Rockford Peaches counterpart, Dorothy Kamenshek, was "the fanciest fielding first baseman I've ever seen—man or woman."[2]

Max Carey, league president and a veteran of thousands of major-

Dorothy Kamenshek smiles in triumph after leaping up to catch a ball.

Just as major-league players often did, a player in the AAGPBL argues with an umpire over a call.

league baseball games, maintained that the best game of baseball he had ever seen was a league championship final game between the Racine Belles and the Rockford Peaches. The game, the sixth in the seven-game series, went into extra innings. Finally, in the bottom of the 14th inning, Sophie Kurys, the league's all-time record holder for stolen bases, slid home from second base on a single by Mae "Betty" Trezza. In recalling the final inning of the game, Kurys said, "I got a base hit, stole second and was on my way to third when Betty Trezza hit it in to right field and I slid home. It was close, but I made it."[3] Kury's second base steal was her 201st of the 1946 season, a record for stolen bases unequalled in baseball history. Nearly 6,000 fans watched that contest along with Carey, proving that good baseball, whether played by men or by women, could bring out a crowd. It was this high caliber of play that Meyerhoff banked on when he bought the league.

Eager for more teams and more fans, Meyerhoff expanded the league, beginning with his first season as owner. That year, 1945, he added Fort Wayne and Grand Rapids to the league roster. With the war still raging, three times as many fans paid to see the teams play in the 1945 season as had watched in 1943. For Meyerhoff, the league was a success.

By August 1945 the teams were heading for the playoffs, with the Rockford Peaches on their way to their first league championship. Then, on August 14, V–J Day—marking victory over the Japanese—was declared. The war had ended in Europe in June, and now, with the dropping of the atomic bomb and the surrender of the Japanese, World War II in the Pacific had also come to an end.

With the end of the war thousands of American men were discharged from the armed forces. They needed jobs. The public relations effort that had urged women to leave their homes and families to work in the wartime factories went into reverse. Rosie the Riveter, so recently a heroine, was now regarded as un-American if she did not return to her "rightful" place at home and give up her job to the men who had served overseas. Many companies laid off workers, in part because the end of the war brought a slowdown in heavy industry. In most cases, the first workers to be fired were women. By 1946, millions of American women had lost their jobs. In some companies the Depression-era policy of not hiring married women was reinstated. As women left the workforce, the image of woman's role as homemaker was reintroduced.

The end of the war ushered in an uncertain time for the women's baseball league. After all, Wrigley had founded the first teams as a wartime measure, to compensate for the shortage of men to play ball during the war. Now that the war was over, plenty of male players would be available for the major leagues and for minor-league farm teams. Would there be any place for the women baseball players of the AAGPBL? Just as women were being asked to leave the factories to make room for returning veterans, it seemed that women were expected to leave the world of baseball as well.

Ironically, this occurred just when the league was attracting more and more serious attention from the sports world. Fans and franchises were increasing. At the height of the league's growth, ten ball clubs were playing in front of one million fans per season. *The Baseball Blue Book*, an annual compendium of baseball statistics, included pages on women's baseball for the first time. The editor, Earl Moss, had decided that "girls' baseball was not just another version of softball."[4]

In analyzing the game, he found that the plays at all the bases, especially because of the high incidence of stealing, kept the fans watching the action on many parts of the field at once. He found in comparing the Fort Wayne Daisies to two local men's teams that there was "a larger proportion of runners left on bases to runs scored" in Daisies games "than in standard baseball practice. . . . It brought about a continual pressure and movement toward the plate—an around the diamond threat."[5] This "around the diamond threat" gave the fans plenty to watch for and made the games exciting.

Moss noted one other positive aspect of women's baseball. He main-

Despite fast-paced action and thrilling plays, interest in the AAGPBL began to die out after World War II ended.

tained that in Fort Wayne the Daisies had "produced more sand-lot activity . . . among both boys and girls, than any influence of the last 25 years."[6]—including men's baseball.

In searching for a justification to keep the league going after the war, Meyerhoff picked up on this last angle. The teams were now billed as ways to help prevent juvenile delinquency. It was not that the women who played might otherwise have become juvenile delinquents, but rather that in all of the league cities youngsters made up a large percentage of the fans. With the team members acting as positive role models, league games and league fan clubs gave adolescents of both sexes something constructive to do. Young fans were urged to join clubs called Knot Hole Gangs.

Dorothy Maguire takes a swing.

These clubs were named for the longtime practice of kids who didn't have the price of admission watching ball games through the knot holes in the fences around the ballparks. Membership in a Knot Hole Gang entitled youngsters to attend games at a reduced price.

The league also began to develop kids' teams made up of both boys and girls. These teams played ball according to league rules. They provided kids with healthy alternatives to hanging out on street corners.

A tremendous side effect of this campaign was that the league players provided wonderful role models for young women. As one of the junior players from Fort Wayne put it, "The women were my heroes. They were wonderful role models. I saw strong, risk-taking women as I grew up and that helped me to know it was okay to be a strong, risk-taking and competitive person myself."[7] AAGPBL members who raised children of their own found that their sons as well as their daughters thought highly of their mothers' accomplishments and wanted to be like them. Casey Candaele, a Houston Astros infielder, was proud to be compared to his mother, Helen St. Aubin, who as outfielder Helen Callaghan Candaele was the 1945 league batting champion. An obituary for his mother noted that "Mrs. St. Aubin's stance and swing are almost perfectly preserved in her son Casey Candaele."[8]

As the postwar 1940s unfolded, the league's game more and more closely resembled the game of hardball played in the male major leagues. Although most people, including league owner Meyerhoff, thought this made the game more exciting, it also created a new problem. Recruiting players with the right kind of experience to play the new game effectively was difficult.

In the early days league recruiters would scout municipal and factory softball teams and invite the best players to spring training, where they would compete for spots on the teams. It was relatively simple for good softball players to adjust to the longer base paths and the lead-off and base-stealing changes that Wrigley had first made. By 1948, however, the former softball players also had to adjust to a smaller ball and an overhand pitch. Two weeks of spring training was often too little time for players to make these adjustments.

The switch to hardball rules and overhand throwing was particularly hard for pitchers. Some, like underhand pitching champion Connie Wisniewski of the Grand Rapids Chicks, were valuable enough at the plate to be able to play another position and retain their spot on the team. Pitching overhand was more exhausting and more physically hazardous than underhand pitching. No longer could a pitcher last all the innings of a doubleheader. It was even unwise for a pitcher to pitch every day.

As a result, more pitchers were needed for each team. Starting in 1948, the leading hurlers pitched about half the number of innings as had their predecessors.

The changes in the game did not upset the baseball purists who owned and managed the teams. The rules for baseball as played by the men in the National League and the American League had evolved slowly over the course of nearly 100 years of professional play, and they continued to evolve. There were even some minor rule differences in the way the game was played by the two major leagues. At the beginning of the 1947 season, *Newsweek* declared that in a few years the AAGPBL "has gone farther than organized baseball did in its first ten."[9] And Max Carey echoed, "It has taken men's baseball fifty years to settle on its distances and rules. We have made tremendous strides . . . and feel that we are well on our way to accomplishing our aims—to bring about the best looking sports spectacle in as short a time as possible."[10]

For the men in charge of the league, making "tremendous strides" meant expansion. At the same time, more teams meant that even more players were needed. In 1946 the Muskegon Lassies and the Peoria Red-wings joined the league. They were followed in 1948 for a single season by teams from Chicago and Springfield. The Muskegon team switched to Kalamazoo in 1950, and the Battle Creek Belles picked up the Racine fran-chise in 1951, finishing the league's lineup. All in all, more than 600 women would eventually work as salaried players on 15 teams. (There were never more than 10 franchises operating at a time.)

With the recruitment of players becoming more difficult, the teams were often uneven. For a powerhouse team like Rockford to play the newly formed Chicago Colleens in 1948, for example, was not very exciting ball. To counter this, the men at league headquarters shuffled players around in an attempt to balance the teams with a combination of strong and weak players. However, since the players and the home cities identified with each other, trading of popular players angered both teams and fans. At the beginning of each season during the postwar years, teams were told they could retain only ten players. The other five were reassigned by the head office in an attempt to even the competition. During midseason, especially when an expansion team was in trouble, other trades were made, whether the teams or traded players wanted them or not.

To help the struggling Chicago Colleens, for example, the Grand Rapids Chicks were required to trade them either Ernestine Petra, their star shortstop, or Alma Ziegler, their captain. As Dottie Hunter, a member of the Chicks put it, "Well, Zig was captain and had been forever. So Teeny had to go."[11] Many of the greatest players in the league were inextricably identified with their teams. It would be hard to determine the extent to which fans' support made heroines out of South Bend's Bonnie Baker, Rockford's Dottie Kamenshek, or Racine's Joanne Winter and Sophie Kurys.

One positive result of the need for more recruits was greater diversity among the players. During spring training in 1947, Meyerhoff sent nearly 200 players to Havana. Earlier that spring the Brooklyn Dodgers had worked out in Cuba, convinced that their new rookie, Jackie Robinson, would be better off training outside the racist American South, where teams traditionally had held spring training. Cuba, a country devoted to baseball, provided the league with thousands of fans for exhibition games. Beginning in 1947, Cuba also provided the league with new recruits.

Many of these recruits came from a women's league founded by a wealthy Cuban, Rafael de Leon, and patterned after the AAGPBL. To the relatively poor Cuban players, American baseball promised a chance to emigrate to a richer country, where they could make a better living. After spring training in 1947, Eulalia Gonzales joined the Racine Belles, becoming the first Cuban to play in the AAGPBL. Over the next few years many other players came to the United States from Cuba, among them Gloria Ruiz, Ysora Castillo, Mirtha Marrero, Adeline Garcia, and Isabel Alvarez. Alvarez, perhaps the most successful of the Cuban players, first pitched for the Fort Wayne Daisies. After that she played for Kalamazoo, Grand Rapids, and Battle Creek, ending her career in Fort Wayne in the last season of the league's existence. She became an American citizen and remained in the United States after the league folded.

The recruitment problems of the late 1940s were not readily apparent. With a million fans in attendance at league games and ten franchises in 1948, the venture seemed to be a huge success. But too many teams depended on aging veterans. Excitement dwindled as the Rockford Peaches dominated season after season. The economy didn't help. The small cities that had thrived during the war suffered with the end of the war industries. There was widespread unemployment in the factories of Rockford, South Bend, Racine and Muskegon.

The first season of the new decade brought serious changes to the league and foreshadowed the end of women's professional baseball. The Muskegon Lassies collapsed before the season ended, although Kalamazoo picked up the franchise. At the end of the 1950 season Racine, which had been home to the Belles since the beginning, gave up its franchise to Battle Creek, Michigan.

These changes, plus increasing debt, put pressure on Meyerhoff. In 1950 he sold his interest in the league to local backers in each of the remaining franchise cities. Small businessmen had backed the league from the beginning. They believed that mismanagement in the central office had led to the league's financial troubles, and they were eager to manage the individual teams on their own.

But the downward spiral continued in spite of the change in management. By the spring of 1954 only five teams were left—Kalamazoo, South Bend, Rockford, Grand Rapids and Fort Wayne. They managed to field teams but at reduced salaries. Umpires no longer worked outside their hometowns in order to reduce expenses. On some teams the chaperones doubled as players.

In early September the final game was played, with Kalamazoo upsetting Fort Wayne for the 1954 championship.

The failure of the league can be blamed as much on changes in society as on problems with league management. The league had begun with a powerful publicity campaign aimed at showing that women and baseball were not only compatible, but patriotic. The league's final years coincided with an era in which it was no longer considered fashionable or patriotic for women to work in traditional male fields—or even to work outside the home at all.

The 1950s were an extremely conservative period in American history, especially socially and politically. The war was over. The need for women in the workforce ended with the dropping of the atomic bomb on Japan— or so the argument went. "Real women" would want to leave the factories and go back home and have babies as soon as they could. A new film produced by the government at the end of the war showed Rosie the Riveter in her factory, but instead of talking about her work, she declared that she had only been holding a job until her husband returned. Once he came back, she vowed she would go back to housekeeping, where she belonged.

The late 1940s and early 1950s saw such an incredible growth in the U.S. population that the babies born in this time period would come to be called baby boomers. Women were told there was no greater job than to have these babies and then to stay home and feed and diaper them.

Conventional medical opinion viewed pregnancy as an illness. It was widely believed that women should not work—let alone play ball—if they were pregnant. Most members of the league, in fact, retired from baseball when they began having children. A notable exception was Dottie Collins, a pitcher for the Fort Wayne Daisies. At the beginning of the 1948 season Collins had discovered that she was pregnant. She refused to quit and pitched well into the sixth month of her pregnancy.

Over four million babies were born in 1954 alone. It had taken a powerful propaganda campaign, short skirts, and Helena Rubinstein to make women's baseball socially acceptable in 1943. It would have taken an even more powerful campaign to keep spectators coming in the 1950s. As one player put it, "We were going against society, with its rules and regulations telling us that this is the way we should grow up and this is what we should do."[12]

The league, however, had provided a different model of growing up for young girls who liked baseball. As short-lived as it was, it lasted long enough for a girl to go to the league games, watch her heroines play ball, and grow old enough to play professional ball herself. This was the case for Marilyn Jenkins. As a batgirl for Grand Rapids in the 1940s, she dreamed of playing in the league when she grew up. She realized her dream, becoming a catcher for the Grand Rapids team. She later recalled, "I was bat girl until I was sixteen. . . . Then, when I was seventeen, I started playing. It would have been the disappointment of my life had I not become a player."[13]

For Marilyn Jenkins and a handful of other girls growing up in the 1940s, the opportunity to play major-league baseball existed, if only for a short time. It would be two decades before girls would play organized baseball again.

Chapter 5

LITTLE LEAGUE: ALL-AMERICAN BOYS

. . . AND GIRLS

In addition to battling the changing social mores, the organizers of the AAGPBL had increasing difficulties recruiting new players. One of the reasons for the demise of the league was the scarcity of players with the necessary hardball experience. Little girls, with the rare exception of those few living in league cities with junior teams, had no opportunity to play hardball. Boys, on the other hand, could play Little League ball, a miniature version of major-league baseball. Little League, a program begun in 1939 in Williamsport, Pennsylvania, had rapidly spread throughout the country and the world. By 1974 the Little League Baseball organization was overseeing 2.25 million boys on 9,100 baseball teams in 31 countries; 80 percent of these boys were in the United States. The charter, officially sanctioned by Congress, limited participation to boys.

For boys, Little League was the first step on the way to fulfilling their dreams of making it to the major leagues. By 1993, 75 percent of all major-league players had started their careers as Little Leaguers. Boston Red Sox great Carl Yastrzemski was the first Little Leaguer to make it all the way to the Hall of Fame. Little League teams had all the trappings of major-league ball—uniforms, local business support, major- and minor-league divisions (based on age), and state and national championships. As Felicia Lee, a 12-year-old who was one of the earliest female players allowed into Little League, said, "Girls' softball isn't nearly as much fun. In Little League you get to play hardball; you get to play more games; and they give you uniforms and trophies."[1]

If a boy wanted a life of competitive baseball, Little League was a logical training ground for such a career. Many girls wanted to be part of this training because they, too, wanted to be major-league players when they grew up. As the president of the American Women's Baseball Association put it, "Hey, little girls who go to Wrigley Field have the same dreams as little boys. We want to grow up and play baseball."[2] As early as the 19th century, the famous feminist Elizabeth Cady Stanton had said, "We cannot say what the woman might be physically, if the girl were allowed all the freedom of the boy, in romping, swimming, climbing and playing ball."[3] Excluding girls from Little League limited girls' options and narrowed their opportunities for development as baseball players.

Until 1957, Little League rules did not expressly forbid girls from playing in Little League. But in 1956 and 1957, several girls tried to join Little League teams. Although these girls were few in number and represented no threat to organized baseball, specific language excluding girls was added to the official Little League regulations.

These girls were viewed as talented tomboys whose interest in baseball was likely to wane as soon as adolescence set in. If they could play good baseball, they were usually tolerated by their male teammates and coaches. One such girl was Connie Lawn, who played second base for a Long Beach, California, team in 1956. She recalled in 1971, "The highlight of my career was hitting a bases loaded home run off the town bully."[4]

Another pioneer was Nancy Lotsey, of Morristown, New Jersey, who was the only girl on her Small Fry League team. A pitcher, Nancy struck out three batters and won the game in her 1963 pitching debut.

Until the 1970s, however, such efforts to integrate children's baseball were limited to a few individual girls who tried out or played for local teams, usually without much fanfare. In the early 1970s girls in larger numbers began to express an interest in playing ball. They, their parents, and feminists realized that excluding girls from Little League limited their options and narrowed their opportunities for development as baseball players. Throughout the late 1960s and into the early 1970s, women in the United States had become increasingly angry about inequities that they perceived throughout American society—in employment, in salaries, and in social customs and practices.

Sports were a logical target for organizations like the National Organization for Women (NOW). The majority of NOW members agreed with Carol Forbes, an activist who helped integrate girls into the national Soapbox Derby competition. Forbes argued, "Sports is vital in determining aggressiveness and competition in life, and of course, the men want to buy it off with separate but equal. . . . The failure to compete with men in sports infiltrates every facet of our lives."[5]

In the 1970s girls and women did not want what the women of the AAGPBL had wanted—a chance for women to play their own game of baseball. The feminist movement encouraged girls and women to participate in areas that had previously been the province of boys and men. Girls and women were eager to have equal opportunities to compete with boys and men on turf that had been closed to females. Baseball had long been exclusively male turf. It was the national pastime.

The importance of baseball in American culture as reflected in the pervasiveness of baseball terms in American language. "Striking out," "getting to first," "going all the way," "hitting one out of the park," and "hitting a grand slam" were all phrases used by American men to describe deals they made in every arena from finance to romance. Feminists argued that a disproportionate amount of the nation's power and wealth were controlled by men, who because of custom and practice such as Little League's "boys only" rule that pervaded all levels of society, had common opportunities that girls would never have. As one civil rights commissioner put it, "Little League is as American as hot dogs and apple pie. There's no reason why that part of Americana should be withheld from girls."[6]

By 1972, the U.S. government appeared to agree. In that year Public Law 92-318 went into effect. Part of this law was Title IX of the Education Amendments, which made it illegal for any recipient of federal funds to discriminate on the basis of sex. Women in college and university athletic departments across the country rejoiced. For years athletic budgets for women's teams had ranked far below those of men's teams. Most colleges and universities received federal funds of some sort, through research grants or scholarships. Women's athletic directors interpreted the new law as meaning that their budgets and programs had to equal those of their male counterparts or the schools would lose federal funds.

Prior to the passage of Title IX, the statistics were stark. At one state university in the Northwest, where 40 percent of the student body was women, less than 2 percent of the total $2 million athletic budget— $40,000—was spent on women's programs. At a large midwestern university the men's budget was 1,300 times greater than the budget for women's sports. And it was typical at smaller colleges for men's teams to be fully funded while women's teams held bake sales and car washes to raise money for team travel and uniforms.

With the passage of Title IX, the climate changed. Women's organizations seized upon the spirit of the new law to attack discrimination everywhere, even in groups that were not directly affected by the law. Little League was a natural target for feminists—and for little girls who wanted to play baseball. The first of the would-be Little Leaguers to gain national

Maria Pepe, the first young woman to go to court to fight for the right to play Little League baseball

attention was Maria Pepe. In 1972 Maria was selected to play on a team in Hoboken, New Jersey. Her teammates were glad to have her because 11-year-old Maria was a good ballplayer. However, the national Little League headquarters said the Hoboken team would be expelled from the league if it kept a girl on its roster. With the help of feminist activists who believed that girls should have the same opportunities as boys, Maria and her parents went to court. Eventually, she won, but by the time the case was settled, Maria was 13, too old for Little League.

While Maria Pepe was struggling to break into Little League in New Jersey, girls in other parts of the country were making similar efforts. In 1973 in Ypsilanti, Michigan, 12-year-old Carolyn King joined one of Ypsilanti's Little League teams. The national Little League organization promptly threatened to throw Ypsilanti out of the organization. The Ypsi-

Carol and Renate Gygi look proudly at a picture of Carolyn King, whose case prompted Carol to take on the Little League team in Portland, Oregon, so that Renate could play.

lanti Orioles, with the backing of city officials, kept fighting. They did not want to lose a good center fielder. The city managers sided with Carolyn. They announced that the city's ballparks could not be used by any team that discriminated against girls. As Carolyn said at the hearing, "When the order came from national Little League headquarters that the Orioles had to drop me, my coaches . . . really stuck by me. So did the city council. . . . But the team lost its charter, so now we're not in Little League anymore. We're a youth league funded by the city, and we're open to all boys and girls. I'm sure glad that women are finally getting their rights."[7]

Other girls were not as lucky. They did not have the support of their coaches and communities. In Haverhill, Massachusetts, for example, Sharon Poole joined the Haverhill Indians. In the two games she was allowed to play before being ejected from the league (her coach was also

Sharon Poole played alongside her little brother Mike on her Little League team until she was kicked off and her coach was fired for letting her play.

fired), Sharon helped win both games by batting cleanup and playing errorless ball at center field. At the end of Sharon's career, a fellow player, a nine-year-old first baseman, observed that the ballplayers "didn't care, but their mothers and fathers did."[8] In an editorial supporting Sharon's case, the *Boston Globe* seconded the boy's analysis: "Obviously a parent may lose his or her sense of self-importance if some girl strikes out his or her son, or hits a homer off him, or throws him out at second."[9] For Sharon the situation was simple: She was kicked out "just because I was a girl."[10]

In other parts of the country, the story was the same. Yvonne Burch, a 13-year-old slugger, joined the South Cabarrus Optimists in Concord, North Carolina. The Optimists were a team in the Babe Ruth League, a baseball organization for boys aged 13 to 18. The Babe Ruth League was as adamantly opposed to girls joining them as was the Little League. When the national headquarters threatened to suspend all the teams in Concord if Yvonne continued to play, the local teams gave in.

Yvonne told the story this way: "I did pretty good on the team. The only razzing I got was from the stands. . . . [Then] one day some man from Trenton threatened to cancel the club's Babe Ruth League charter, so I had to leave the team."[11] Yvonne stressed that she wanted to play hardball, not softball. "There's an all girls softball league around here, but it's stupid. They make you use an underhand pitch, and they don't let you steal or slide. They take all the fun out of the game just because they think it's too rough for girls."[12]

In spite of these individual setbacks, the push to include girls in Little League was gathering momentum throughout 1972 and 1973. Ellen Vetromile of Ho-Ho-Kus, New Jersey; Dorothy Dombrowski of Redondo Beach, California; Dierdre Fitzgerald of Stony Brook, New York; Jenny Fuller of Mill Valley, California; Frances Pescatore of Ridgefield, New Jersey; and Kim Green of Wilmington, Delaware (whose father, Dallas, was a former major leaguer)—all pressed for girls' rights to play ball.

Robert Stirrat, the Little League vice president, stated the league's position: "Baseball is traditionally a boys' game. To admit girls would certainly cripple the program."[13] Many people and groups disagreed, including girl ballplayers, their parents, and NOW.

Because of a decision by a New Jersey judge, Sylvia Pressler, young women like Julie Spencer and those whose pictures follow in the next few pages were allowed to play the game they love on Little League teams around the United States.

The critical battle took place in New Jersey. Acting on behalf of a complaint from several young female ballplayers, Judge Sylvia Pressler, an examination officer with the New Jersey Division on Civil Rights, ordered the Little League in New Jersey to allow girls to play in the fall of 1973. The case was appealed to a three-judge panel of the Appellate Division of the New Jersey Superior Court.

One Houston, Texas, Little League official observed, "It was a lady-judge who ruled in favor of the girls. It hasn't moved up to male judges yet."[14] When it did, the Houston official, like many others in Little League, would be sorely disappointed. The verdict from the appellate division once again favored the girls. Upon hearing the verdict, Robert Stirrat, the Little League official, said "we assumed" that most people "accepted baseball as

Anne-Marie Sandquist of Denver, Colorado, whose coach said she was the best player on her team

a male prerogative."[15] He was wrong. Prerogatives based on gender alone were no longer acceptable, at least in Little League.

The arguments before the appellate court had focused on two things: the alleged physical danger to girls in playing baseball and the civil rights of girls being excluded from baseball. The Little League argued that girls were weaker than boys, that girls were more prone to injuries than boys, that breast cancer could be caused by girls being hit in the chest by baseballs, and that "because of their social roles" girls had more to lose from cosmetic injuries than boys.

The advocates for the girls called medical experts to testify. They directly refuted the first three charges. Dr. Joseph Torg, a pediatric ortho-

Penny Clemo of Portland, Oregon, considered by coaches and players the best pitcher in her league

pedic surgeon who worked as a consultant for the Philadelphia 76ers basketball team, testified that girls' bones tended to be more resistant to injury than those of boys. No compelling evidence was offered to support the league's claim that "cancerous lesions may be produced by traumatic impact upon female breast tissue."[16] As to the league contention that girls had to be specially protected from facial injuries because of their social roles, the courts found that this was a matter of social custom. The argument lacked medical proof.

During the controversy, most parents agreed with Betty Hoadley, the mother of would-be Little Leaguer Kristen Hoadley, who was asked which of her children—her son or her daughter—she would rather have lose a tooth in baseball. "Either," she replied. "They are equal human beings."[17] And Dallas Green weighed in with the opinion: "For kids under 12, baseball should be fun for everybody, and it shouldn't matter if girls play."[18] Perhaps the final word on physical risk came from a ten-year-old male Little Leaguer, Tom Thornton, who told a reporter succinctly, "If girls are good, they won't get hurt."[19]

Ultimately, the decision was made on the grounds of civil rights. The New Jersey court ruled that Little League ball clubs fell under the definition of "places of public accommodation."[20] As such they could not discriminate on the basis of race or gender under federal and state civil rights legislation. The panel ruled that Little League was a "public accommodation because the invitation to play is open to children in the community at large with no restriction (other than sex) whatever. It is public in the added sense that characteristically, local governmental bodies make the playing areas available to the local leagues, ordinarily without charge."[21] Since Little League was the only game in town, girls had to be allowed to play.

The final ruling by the New Jersey court was handed down in March 1974, just in time for spring tryouts. The Little League organization, under pressure from the courts, from parents, and from the women's movement, announced in the spring that girls as well as boys could play Little League baseball. In Tenafly, New Jersey, nine-year-old Amy Dickinson was the number one draft choice among 150 players. That same month hundreds of women formed a Mothers' March on Washington to ensure that what had happened in New Jersey would happen all over the United States.

An informal poll of two major-league teams—the New York Mets and the New York Yankees—found widespread support for the integration of girls into Little League. There were some notable exceptions, however. New York Mets manager Yogi Berra growled, "Let them play softball. God made us different."[22] And shortstop Fritz Peterson complained, "Why should a girl take a guy's place?"[23] More typical, however, was the reaction of former Little Leaguer Elliot Maddox, whose hometown, Union, New Jersey, had a long history of producing good male ballplayers. "What," said Maddox, "says guys are the only ones who are supposed to have fun?"[24]

In spite of a few spoilers, on June 7, 1974, when the first game of the new season was played, girls were in the lineup.

Congresswoman Martha W. Griffith, a Michigan Democrat, introduced legislation in the House of Representatives to amend the national charter of the Little League organization. With the mothers' support, the House rapidly voted to change the charter. A few months later the Senate concurred. On a motion from Republican Senator Roman Hruska, the national charter of the Little League was amended. "Young people" was substituted for "boys," and the development of "manhood" was stricken from the list of the league's purposes. On December 26, 1974, President Gerald Ford signed the bill into law.

Twenty years after the demise of the All-American Girls Professional Baseball League, girls once again had an opportunity to play hardball.

Jackie Adams of Attleboro, Massachusetts, proved she could outplay all the boys to win a spot on her team.

In 1984, Victoria Roche became the first girl to take part in the Little League World Series, playing as a member of the team from Europe.

Chapter 6

A LEAGUE
OF THEIR OWN

OR A PLACE
ON THE TEAM?

I n her affidavit for the New Jersey court explaining why she wanted to play ball like her best friend, Rocco Umbrino, Frances Pescatore wrote, "I am eleven years old, and therefore three years of my career have been wasted."[1] Looking at the history of women's baseball over the last 50 years, it would be easy to make light of young Frances' concern. Certainly there was little probability of a real career ahead for her in major-league baseball.

And yet, Frances' testimony hit at the crux of the matter. For most of the time since baseball was invented and became an American passion, girls and women have been excluded from playing the game at the same level as boys and men. The one shining exception was the 12 years that the AAGPBL played ball.

As short-lived as that time was, no other professional team sport for women has lasted as long. Since the adoption of Title IX, women's professional leagues in softball, basketball, and volleyball have all been founded and then have folded. All have lacked what Wrigley was able to give the AAGPBL. He, with Art Meyerhoff, was able to capitalize on public opinion about expanding women's roles at a time when the nation was extraordinarily unified in facing an outside threat. In the age of Rosie the Riveter, "Rosie the Center Fielder" seemed a natural.

Secondly, and as important, Wrigley gathered financial support and media attention for his teams. Any women's league today must battle for a share of the multimillion-dollar business represented by media support of major male athletic events. Women's tennis, golf, and some Olympic events have come a long way in the past 20 years in terms of prize money and network coverage, but no women's team sport has been able to crack the television monopoly of the National Football League, National and American (Baseball) Leagues, National Basketball Association, or even the National Hockey League.

The women of the AAGPBL were unique in the history of women's baseball because they played exclusively with women on all-women's teams. They might not, however, have gained the full support of modern feminists. On the one hand, the women's movement has given a huge boost to women's athletics and has raised public consciousness about the role of sports and physical fitness for women. In a 1988 survey of American parents, 87 percent believed that sports were as important for girls as for boys. Eighty percent of the girls surveyed said that they believed that boys like girls who play sports, laying to rest the myth that a "tomboy" will never have a date.[2]

At the same time, however, feminist thinking has been conflicted on the issue of whether girls should play sports together without boys or whether true equality can only come when teams are coed. The latter argument fueled the battle with the Little League. However, it never crossed Philip Wrigley's mind for an instant that the way to fill out teams depleted by the war was to sign Toni Stone or Babe Didrikson Zaharias to the Chicago Cubs.

Nor is coed playing the only issue for women's sports. In spite of Title IX, college athletic budgets are still unequal. A National Collegiate Athletic Association report at the beginning of the 1990s found that although young women account for at least half the college population, less than 25 percent of the money spent on college athletics is spent on women's teams and programs. At every level, from Olympic competition to junior high, girls and women have far fewer sports opportunities than boys and men. This is true in spite of phenomenal growth in women's participation in sports. For example, in 1971, 294,000 girls were playing high-school sports; in 1992, two million. As Donna Lopiano, executive director of the Women's Sports Foundation, remarked, "Sports in our society is still a right for little boys and a privilege for little girls."[3]

One little girl who tried to make it to the major leagues was Julie Croteau. A Little League player from the age of six (two years after girls were admitted), Julie was an excellent first baseman whose parents, both attorneys, fought at each step of her career for her inclusion on boys' teams. Julie believed that her experience was not equal to that of the boys with whom she played. She explained, "As we got older, the coaches didn't see the girls as having any future in the game and didn't work as hard with them as with the guys."[4] In spite of this lack of attention, Julie kept playing the game she loved and finally earned a place on her college team amid much national media attention. At the end of three seasons, however, she hung up her spikes, saying simply, "I'm miserable."[5] Although her teammates treated her well, she did not enjoy being on a team whose teammates routinely made insulting sexual remarks about other women. Although never aimed at her, they were exclusionary and discriminatory; in short, she found it uncomfortable to be "one of the boys."

Another pioneer on boys' teams, Carey Schueler, daughter of former major-league pitcher Ron Schueler, is sticking with her career. The first female pitcher on a high-school team in California, Carey was named Freshman Player of the Year in 1990 in a statewide poll. She maintains, "Most of the guys on the team just think it doesn't matter whether I'm a girl or not."[6]

To the founders and players of the AAGPBL, still the most successful women's baseball organization, it did matter that they were "girls." Although the world of sports has moved a long way from the time when the Greeks threw women over cliffs just for watching athletic contests, full equality has yet to be achieved. Baseball makes an interesting test case. U.S. baseball is fraught with myth and emotion and is a bastion of exclusionary male bonding. The inclusion of women in the major leagues would clearly mark a major milestone in the equality of the sexes.

Whether that goal is to be achieved by women playing on teams in a women's league or by individual women playing on predominantly male teams remains to be seen. Clearly, the women's teams of the AAGPBL came closest to gaining popular acceptance of women playing baseball. Their role in history should be remembered as more than a footnote in the annals of baseball.

★ ★ ★

A display at the National Baseball Hall of Fame and Museum in Cooperstown, New York, honors the achievements of the players of the AAGPBL.

NOTES

Chapter 1

1. Billie Jean King with Frank Deford, *Billie Jean* (New York: Viking, 1982), p. 12.

2. Mabel Lee, *A History of Physical Education and Sports in the United States* (New York: Wiley, 1983), p. 58.

3. Helen Lenskyj, *Out of Bounds: Women, Sport and Sexuality* (Toronto: The Women's Press, 1986), p. 12.

4. Donald Laird, "Why Aren't More Women Athletes?" *Scientific American* (March 1936), p. 143.

5. Barbara Gregorich, *Women at Play: The Story of Women in Baseball* (New York: Harcourt, Brace, 1993), p. 3.

6. Ibid.

7. Ibid., p. 14.

8. Ibid., p. 51.

9. Ibid., p. 75.

Chapter 2

1. Lois Browne, *Girls of Summer: The Real Story of the All-American Girls' Professional Baseball League* (Toronto: HarperCollins, 1992), pp. 12–13.

2. "Baseball: Babette Ruths," *Newsweek* (June 24, 1947), p. 68.

3. Browne, p. 25.

4. Ibid., p. 35.

5. Ibid., p. 52.

6. Jack Fischer, "When the Diamond Was a Girl's Best Friend," *Smithsonian* (July 1989), p. 92.

7. Ibid.

8. Browne, p. 53.

9. Sue Macy, *A Whole New Ballgame: The Story of the All-American Girls Professional Baseball League* (New York: Henry Holt, 1993), p. 10.

10. Ibid.

Chapter 3

1. Lenskyj, p. 11.

2. Allen Guttman, *Women's Sports: A History* (New York: Columbia University Press, 1991), p. 145.

3. Jerry D. Lewis, "The Girls of Summer," *Sport* (August 1990), p. 14.

4. "Baseball: Babette Ruths," p. 68.

5. Ibid., p. 69.

6. "Play Ball," *Time* (June 1943), p. 62.

7. "Baseball: Babette Ruths," p. 68.

8. Lewis, p. 14.

9. Fischer, p. 93.

10. Ibid., p. 93.

11. Ibid., p. 91.

12. Browne, p. 45.

13. Ibid., p. 45.

14. "Girls' Baseball," *Life* (June 4, 1945), p. 63.

15. Macy, p. 17.

16. Ibid., p. 18.

17. Gregorich, p. 125.

18. Fischer, p. 88.

19. Browne, p. 41.

20. Gregorich, p. 88.

21. Fischer, p. 91.

22. Browne, p. 48.

23. Macy, p. 78.

24. Browne, p. 94.

Chapter 4

1. Gregorich, p. 67.

2. Lewis, p. 14.

3. Fischer, p. 91.

4. Browne, p. 103.

5. Ibid., p. 104.

6. Ibid.

7. Macy, p. 103.

8. Robert McG. Thomas, Jr., "Helen C. St. Aubin, Athlete Inspired Movies," *New York Times* (December 11, 1992), p. D19.

9. "Baseball: Babette Ruths," p. 69.

10. Browne, p. 153.

11. Ibid., p. 152.

12. Macy, p. 98.

13. Browne, p. 93.

Chapter 5

1. Letty Cottin Pogrebin, "Baseball Diamonds Are a Girl's Best Friend," *Ms.* (September 1974), p. 82.

2. Michael Kiefer, "Hardball," *Women's Sports and Fitness* (April 1992), p. 56.

3. Roberta J. Park, "Sport, Gender and Society in a Transatlantic Victorian Perspective," in J. A. Mangan and Roberta J. Park, eds., *From 'Fair Sex' to Feminism: Sport and the Socialization of Women in the Industrial and Post-Industrial Eras* (London: Frank Cass, 1987), p. 66.

4. Connie Lawn, Letter to editor, *New York Times* (July 16, 1971), p. 30.

5. Frank Deford, "Now Georgy-Porgy Runs Away," *Sports*

Illustrated (April 22, 1974), p. 37.

6. "Little League in Jersey Ordered to Allow Girls to Play on Teams," *New York Times* (November 8, 1973), p. 99.

7. Pogrebin, p. 82.

8. "Sharon's Brief Baseball Career—Town Wasn't On Her Side," *New York Times* (July 7, 1971), p. 26.

9. Ibid.

10. Ibid.

11. Pogrebin, p. 82.

12. Ibid.

13. Louise Saul, "Little League Gets a New Umpire—The Courts," *New York Times* (February 24, 1974), p. 63.

14. "Cathy at the Bat," *Newsweek* (April 1, 1974), p. 53.

15. "Girls a Hit in Debut on Diamond," *New York Times* (March 25, 1974), p. 67.

16. "Cathy at the Bat," p. 55.

17. Ibid.

18. Ibid.

19. "Girls a Hit," *New York Times* (March 25, 1974), p. 67.

20. "You Really Hit That One, Man; Said the Little League Boy to the Little League Girl," *New York Times* (May 19, 1974), VI, p. 36.

21. Ibid.

22. "In New Jersey, Little Women Get to 1st Base," *New York Times* (April 2, 1974), VI, p. 8.

23. Ibid.

24. Ibid.

Chapter 6

1. Deford, p. 30.

2. "A Taboo Whose Time Has Gone," *Women's Sports and Fitness* (October/November 1988), p. 56.

3. Susan L. Morse, "Women & Sports," *The CQ Researcher* (March 6, 1992), p. 195.

4. "Interview with Julie Croteau," *Women's Sports and Fitness* (September 1989), p. 64.

5. Morse, p. 197.

6. "Pitcher Perfect," *Women's Sports and Fitness* (July/August 1990), p. 67.

FOR FURTHER READING

Browne, Lois. *Girls of Summer: The Real Story of the All-American Girls' Professional Baseball League*. Toronto: HarperCollins, 1992.

Gregorich, Barbara. *Women at Play: The Story of Women in Baseball*. New York: Harcourt, Brace, 1993.

Guttman, Allen. *Women's Sports: A History*. New York: Columbia University Press, 1991.

King, Billie Jean, with Frank Deford. *Billie Jean*. New York: Viking, 1982.

Lee, Mabel. *A History of Physical Education and Sports in the United States*. New York: Wiley, 1983.

Lenskyj, Helen. *Out of Bounds: Women, Sport and Sexuality*. Toronto: The Women's Press, 1986.

Macy, Sue. *A Whole New Ball Game: The Story of the All-American Girls Professional Baseball League*. New York: Henry Holt, 1993.

Mangan, J. A. and Roberta J. Park, eds. *From 'Fair Sex' to Feminism: Sport and the Socialization of Women in the Industrial and Post-Industrial Eras*. London: Frank Case, 1987.

For a movie version of the history of the AAGPBL, you can watch *A League of Their Own*, starring Geena Davis, Rosie O'Donnell, and Madonna.

INDEX